## POEMS

## IMPERFECTION VERSUS PERFECTION

### AUTHOR AND PHOTOGRAPHY

### KESI M. OMARI

*Cover Designed By Katrina'sWORKS*

This publication is a collection of poetry, designed as pleasurable reading for inspiration.

All rights reserved. No part of this document may be reproduced in any form or by any means without written permission from the author.

~~~~

**IMPERFECTION VERSUS PERFECTION**

Copyright © April 2014

Kesi M. Omari

**In Spirit We Are Broken Working Spiritually To Become Holy**

**Kesi M. Omari**

Is Published Under the Umbrella

of

## Inspirations and Dedications

Inspirations for my work are from my family members, friends, associates, and strangers; from all walks of life. Just to live a life of feeling free, yet so broken, was for me a life of repentance and conversion; enabling me to share my inner most thoughts of imperfections while working toward perfection.

\*\*\*

I dedicate this book to Na'eem Omari, Rose, B.J., Virginia, Bruce, and Rosiland, Printice, Dae, April, Champayne, Autume, and Mr. Sydney and Rosie Taylor.

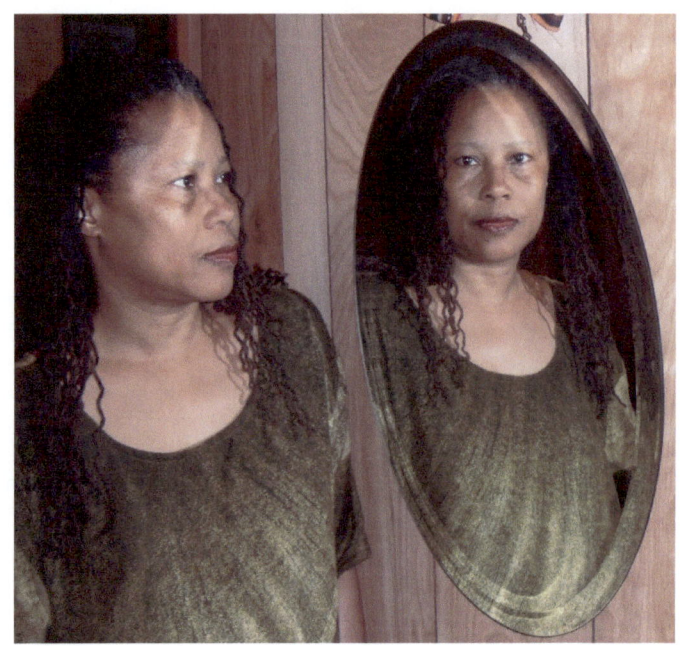

## Total Unity

### (If I Should Die)

Before I wake

Asking you care for my soul

Keep me with you and take me home

There are so many times that I pray knowing my heart is

controlling (my mind) the evil from within to do that

which I know to be wrong that I choose to see as right.

My life is almost somewhere

It could happen today if I keep watching for your errors

I see nothing to acknowledge that I have done

Although, I talk behind your back

And I heard you do it also.

There will be no chances left for me

I will work alone

I can do this by myself

I don't need anyone

I'm going do it my way
My way or no way

Releasing me as I am
Acknowledging all my known sins
Asking God's forgiveness
Repenting
Stopping those sins
Trying to repair what I messed up

Removed emotions
Removed personal views
Removed jealousy
Removed self

Replaced SELF with The Character of Christ
Replaced SELF with The Word of Christ
Replaced SELF with SELFLESS
The PRINCIPLES of love doesn't have emotions, it does express obedience to the Word of God.
Because of our love for God we want to do His will.
I will be able to stand with Total Unity, only if I should die (to SELF).

## My Lord , Oh GOD Almighty

I am asking for your presence and that you hear my prayer. In Christ name, I ask. And that the Holy Spirit take charge and guide me through this day. Thank you Lord for giving me the opportunity to have life another day. I ask that all my sins are forgiven and I thank you for loving me. I am giving myself to you, to use to use for your will. Fix me so that I am fit, able, and strong enough to do your will.

As I sit here, thoughts of what I should be doing, but also thought of what I am doing is getting in the way of your ordered steps for me as a child of GOD. I could be reading and studying your word, but I thinking of what I know to be doing at this time and place. I am praying for what I want to pray for . I should be asking: what is it that you would have me to do Lord on this glorious day that you have made?

I really want to do your will, my Lord, Oh GOD Almighty. I come, here am I, ready, willing and available to start our days work. Lord, use me.

## One Day At A Time

**Gilmore, Arkansas 72339**

**Dec.14, 2010**

**7:35 p.m.**

This is a lonely night, but I'm thinking about my daughters all of them. They are going through trials and tribulations because of my sinful lifestyle before them. I knew better than to act the way I lived my life. My mom and dad taught me better. My parents stressed to me don't do anything ever that you don't want done to you or things that will cause your children to suffer or your family to suffer. I didn't believe they were telling the truth. It was written, those were God's word, Now I see it happening in my life. I feel the pain that my daughters are feeling. It hurt so bad. Life is great for me and my husband. We work at it, we are committed to God, meaning together until death do us part. I've got to reach my girls and apologize for contributing to some of their grief. Only God knows all the wrong I've done and who I did it to. I surrender all, my whole life to God. I know, I still must pay for what I've done. My suffering is not as painful as the hurt I feel and see in my girls' life.

I say to God in Christ name, please have mercy on them girls and their families that they will receive you and bless your name. Lord I ask you put a hedge around my children as you have done for my husband and me. This is hard to do, a real life confession, it will clear the mind and strengthen the heart. There is only room for LOVE in our heart. Hate and love cannot be in the heart at the same time. Sin cannot be in the presence of Christ.

Much time has separated my sisters and me, there has been very little peace between us. Loving them is easy for me because I will not let any discord become a way of life for me. Jesus is the way. Once I thought my family loved me so much and spoiled me in every way, that is why I moved far away, so I could live my life the way I chose to live. They thought I was too small to take care of myself. I was a free spirited person. I lagged in school, sometimes; however, I was smarter than most, but I didn't choose to show it. I knew as much or more than some of my teachers. My family was smart, the girls and boys. It didn't take much for me to catch on.

God blessed me with brains, knowledge, wisdom, and understanding. This is one day at a time to love God and following his word.

## "Where Is My Friend"

Eye kin cee dat "U" r woen uf va cyin.
(I can see that you are one of a kind)

I thought that life was a lake of happiness,
As time passes the lake dries or the water flows away

This is writers block.

Where is my friend
          By Mai
I had a poem in mind
My heart was fluttering
My eyes were blinking rapidly
My cheeks were tightening
I know it's all because; I didn't see you…..
My friend
Where is my friend..
Eye kin cee  dat "U" r woen uf va cyin.
(I can see that you are one of a kind.)

## Working To Save Our Children

The School District is a reality show waiting to become a new series on ABC, NBC, or Showtime on television.
What is the children's role in the show?
The words are spoken everyday thru-out the school year…
Is it for the children? I love the students….No, it's not.
How are you showing love to the children?

Working to Save Our Kids

The cafeteria leaks and roaches crawl on the tables at breakfast and at lunchtime. This is a real feast at your school.

Who are you?
Working to Save Our Kids

There are some serious issues that have been going on for years however, there is not a one who loves the children enough to stand up for them without thinking that their job would be in jeopardy. Now is the time, job or no job. Why would you say, I would speak up but my family got to eat. Several of you have said, I want to but I need my job. The way students are being treated; the ways some of the teachers are being treated, they ways that the Paraprofessionals and custodians are disrespected is the reasons for failure in the students and the low morale of the teachers. It also affects the entire world, one of these days we will wake up and must accept what that generation that we left behind is in charge of…..it could be deadly and unrecoverable.

It is your fault, or is it our fault?

Who are you?
Working to Save Our Kids

Some of issues may affect the top and that's how it filtered its way down to the bottom. The top is caught up in twirls and someone saw the actions/acts. There is a rude awakening when the top is confronted. Now the confronter is in a position to use leverage to do whatever and move on up. Where are the children in all this mess?

Who are you?
Working to Save Our Kids

The truth of the matter is, who really cares about the children? If someone did, it would not have taken this long to address/confront the unselfish individuals working this district. Scratch my back and I'll scratch yours is the Motto for several school districts. There is a statement that says, do not embarrass the district yet, people are committing adultery with co-workers and getting promotions. There should be punishment.
Why are we punishing the students?

Who are you?
Working to Save Our Kids

It's appears that dogs are in this season and have been for many years everywhere. Where are the children in this dog-eat-dog world?
Teachers are passing by turning their heads when student are receiving inappropriate discipline by another teacher. Loving a child is far from the truth.

Who are you?

To know the whole child is to love that child.
Who really love the children as we love our selves?

It couldn't be you because if you did you would be one that would be working to Save Our Kids.

Who are you?
Working to Save Our Kids

## If - What's in a color

It seems to me
That if I were born brown,
The whole world would be brown
And if I were born white,
Then whole world would be born white

It seems to me
That if I were born black
The whole world would be born black
But then the whole world would be in darkness.

Then it came to me, God is colorblind
The world is a rainbow full or colors

It seems to me
The choice of color for mankind is
THE COLOR OF LOVE
Then, GOD is LOVE

## Broken

Under control of sin sick desires are to be me
The outer parts express and make visible the desires of the world.
The choices of mine are opposite to the will of GOD.
How low am I…. Want to be me; sin sick desires are to be me.
Ears to hear, plug are in, stopped up, muffled all sounds.
Lost, dumb founded, however, it is written
The temple is lent and to be reverenced… is defiled and loosely active in actions of devilish, unmoral deeds reflecting a broken relationship with GOD.
I am broken.

## There Is None In Good Health

When we feed on sinful things
We swallow hate
We belch up envy
Then we chock on the WORD.
None is in good health

## Stop Looking At Me

You are pointing at me
Speaking ill word about me
Believing you know what is best for me
Stop looking at me.

You see you
You are sin sick
Knowing you do not know me
Start looking at you
Stop looking at me.

See now, you see it is you who see
It is not me who you see
You are sin sick
Stop looking at me.

## Let's Get Physical

Lead and walk correct
As we stroll
Let it be righteous and in good health
Follow Christ
Let's get physical

The image portrayal should be that as Christ-like character
Let the menu and strides be the impression of good health
It is a blessing to be moving about with the rhythms of God
Let's get physical

Stop talking about what you eat , how many hours you exercise or how much water you drink, because following GOD's Plan will show in your image.
Let's get physical

## The Preacher

### (He shall fall)

When he speaks

His words are twisted

He shall fall

When he directs

His directions are misdirected

When he warns

His warnings are weak

He shall fall

## I Started to But Ended Up Holy

A chocolate candy bar
I started to eat one

A large glass of sweet tea
I started to drink some

A micro mini skirt
I started to wear one

A Holy Bible
I started to read one

A church
I started to attend one

And hell is where I was headed, but
I repented and
I ended up Holy

## Could This Be A Christian

One who would speak harshly to another
Then say, praise the Lord
Could this be a Christian?

One who would bear false witness against a fellow man?
Then say, yea Lord, my God
Could this be a Christian?

One who would cheat in tithes and offerings
Then say, my Lord, my Lord
Could this be a Christian?

One who would love the Lord
Then say, In the name of Jesus, My Savior, your will, direct me
Could this be a Christian?
This could be a Christian

## My Skin

### (Back to the dust)

Under and through

**my skin**

unbearable pain

**my skin**

is shrinking and melting

Squeezing my vital organs

**my skin**

is bursting into flames

**my skin**

is now many ashes

**my skin**

is back to the dust.

## I Am Your Friend and I Love You

There are so many times we… that is you and I
We may have misunderstood a word or two,
But for some unknown reason or reasons
We shut off the **LOVE**
By not being loving or just stop talking to one another
It is both our faults
Because, I could have asked what is wrong or
You could have asked why did you say _____?

There is so much more to talking than speaking
Showing a sincere concern is **LOVING**
**LOVING** is not talking about you
It **LOVES** you enough to ask other for help
It is to converse about **YOU** with **LOVE** and
To solicit help in an attempt to consider Your needs.

A **FRIEND** is there even when you do not want them around
A **FRIEND** will wait until the time is right to talk about a problem that is stewing in your head.

A Friend ***LOVES***, ***GIVING***, ***CARING***, and ***SHARING***

And most of all…

A ***REAL FRIEND*** is always ***FORGIVING***

We may say things, we may over react, we may misunderstand…

But I will ***ALWAYS*** keep you as

My ***FRIEND AND I LOVE YOU***,

Miss Cookie Young

## My Love for You is Second Best

I am crying for help and comfort from You, Lord.
My heart is hungering
My mind is at full tilt
My mouth is filthy
My tongue is flustered

Where are my friends?
My tears are flowing with much weight and it beating me down
My face and my eyes are swollen
My love for You is second best, if at all.

I say exactly what I want to but hardly do all that I can do.
I dream and vision what I should do
I see what You want me to do but
I just make do; cause
My love for You is second best, if at all.

I am planning to, striving to as we all may say
I will do better than I did yesterday

What shall I do or how may I get into heaven, cause;

My love for You is second best, if at all.

## My Time is Shortened

Time is not on my side; it seems to be getting away from me.

The start of the day is preplanned by Him but as time goes on.
The work was redirected and performed at its worst.

Time is not on my side; it seems to be getting away from me.

The prayers to surrender unto GOD were not prayed nor answered,
The guidance for His will and
The leadership for His ship in my life was not asked
The work was redirected and performed at its worst.

Time is not on my side; it seems to be getting away from me.

The weary mornings are dreary and full of tear drops from the stressors of the world

The aching heart is a result of misbehavior and disobedience of willful acts against GOD
The work was redirected and performed at its worst.

Time is not on my side; it seems to be getting away from me.

There is darkness covering my face
There is silence all around
There is no light
My time is shortened.
The work was redirected and performed at its worst.

## To Love A Friend
### (Thank You God for Wanda)

Love does not harbor envy, prejudice nor deceit. Love begat love and only things that are good. Love was visible and shining thru Mrs. Wanda McNeely. An example of goodness, kindness and flourishing with good character. Wanda was one in a million. She was the love of life for many. Wanda did not wait to express her feelings.

Wanda said life could be short lived and the person would never know. Take time to love purely. This was a wakeup call for many. My friend and co-worker never cease to amaze me. She loved her church, her husband and her daughter and her work family. Walking the talk was the way she showed all of us that there is a GOD.

No one could do what she did without having GOD in her heart. I am not saying that she had no faults but, to us we were surely sure of Wanda having the focus that was directed toward God.

Don't wait to say, I love you
Tell the world around you that you appreciate them.

Don't be a snake in the grass, waiting to strike all the loving beings that are willing and ready to assist in making this world a better place to live for all mankind.

My dear smiling Wanda, I didn't wait, I told Wanda that I loved her in many ways. She showed me that the feelings were mutual and that our trusting friendship was real. We spent many hours together at school, going to visit the sick.

Many times at her home and sometimes away from work; we have cried together, but our laughs were much more than that of the cries and we talked about how to create things to make others happy.

Wanda had the gift of happiness and a smile to knock your socks off. She could be telling you off with that smile and you could not respond with anger because you would only see that beautiful smile.

I loved Wanda and God knows how much I did, I am missing her so much but I thank you, God for sending Wanda in my path it enriched my life and my faith in God. Everything done should be to glorify God.

May God Bless and always comfort Tasha and Ray.

To God be the Glory,
Mrs. Omari

You can find more information on

Kesi M. Omari

At

[https://www.facebook.com/Katrinasworks](https://www.facebook.com/Katrinasworks)

[katrinasworks.com](http://katrinasworks.com)

Scan to view my Website!

www.ingramcontent.com/pod-product-compliance
Lightning Source LLC
Chambersburg PA
CBHW041808040426
42449CB00001B/15